KITES

How to Make

...AND...

How to Fly Them.

By

GEORGE J. VARNEY,

Associate Member of the Boston Aeronautical Society.

———

PUBLISHED BY

GEO. H. WALKER & CO.,

160 Tremont Street   Boston, Mass.

ATLASES.

	PRICE			PRICE
Attleboro Town	$10.00	Malden City	.	$15.00
Barnstable County	15.00	Massachusetts State	.	15.00
Beverly City	15.00	Middlesex County	.	15.00
Brookfield, No. B. and		Milton Town	.	15.00
W. B.	10.00	New Bedford City	.	12.00
Essex County	15.00	Northampton Town	.	12.co
Everett City	15.00	Plymouth County	.	15.00
Fall River City	12.00	Spencer Town	.	10.00
Gardner Town	10.00	Springfield City	.	12.00
Greenfield Town	10.00	Taunton City	.	12.00
Haverhill City	15.00	Westfield Town	.	10.00
Holyoke City	12.00	Winchendon Town	.	10.00
Hull Town	12.00			

WALL MAPS.

	PRICE			PRICE
Boston and Surround-		Everett City	.	$7.50
ings	$1.25	Ireland	.	1.00
Boston	5.00	Long Island	.	8.00
Boston and Vicinity	10.00	Maine State	.	5.00
Boston and Vicinity		Massachusetts State	.	8.00
(extended)	20.00	Massachusetts State	.	20.00
Boston Harbor	20.00	Massachusetts State	.	50.00
Boston Metropolitan		New England	.	7.00
District	35.00	New Hampshire	.	5.00
Boston	75.00	New Haven City	.	1.00
Connecticut	5.00	Plymouth County	.	5.00
Essex County	6.00	Vermont State	.	5.00

Send for Descriptive Catalogue.

GEO. H. WALKER & CO.,
LITHOGRAPHERS,
PHOTO-LITHOGRAPHERS, PROCESS CUTS.

Maps and Plans Reproduced.   Send for Estimates.

160 Tremont St., Boston, Mass.
Opp. Boston Common.

Massachusetts Atlas Plates.

POCKET MAPS.

These Twenty-Seven Plates
Together Cover the Entire State

————AND————

show the roads, railroads, streams, ponds, churches, schoolhouses, cemeteries, etc., etc. The road names are given and the quality of each for driving clearly indicated. At each crossing of the railroad by a public road it is shown whether it is a grade crossing or an overhead or underneath bridge. The elevations are given by buff contour lines at every one hundredth foot elevation. The contour in the water along the shore indicates eighteen feet depth at low tide.

No. 1.	Newburyport and Vicinity.	No. 14.	Taunton and Vicinity.
" 2.	Cape Ann.	" 15.	Dedham and South.
" 3.	Lowell, Lawrence and South.	" 16.	Worcester, South.
" 4.	Boston and Vicinity.	" 17.	Worcester, North.
" 5.	Boston Harbor.	" 18.	Fitchburg and Vicinity.
" 6.	Brockton to Duxbury.	" 19.	Athol and Vicinity.
" 7.	Plymouth and West.	" 20.	Amherst and East.
" 8.	Provincetown and South.	" 21.	Springfield and East.
" 9.	Chatham and West.	" 22.	Springfield and West.
" 10.	Nantucket.	" 23.	Northampton and West.
" 11.	Martha's Vineyard.	" 24.	Greenfield and West.
" 12.	Buzzard's Bay.	" 25.	North Adams and Vicinity.
" 13.	New Bedford and Fall River.	" 26.	Pittsfield and Vicinity.
		" 27.	Great Barrington and South.

In ordering mention either the number of the plate or the name of any town in the State. Price, 25 cents, each plate.

————

These maps are for sale by your dealer, or will be sent by mail on receipt of price.

Send for Descriptive Catalogue.

GEO. H. WALKER & CO.,

LITHOGRAPHERS,
PHOTO-LITHOGRAPHERS,
PROCESS CUTS.

Maps and Plans Reproduced.   Send for Estimates.

160 Tremont Street, Boston, Mass.
Opp. Boston Common.

a stone wall, and at last tangling it up in a strong hedge of thorn.

Several years ago the story was current in Kennebec County, Maine, of a boy who succeeded in launching into the air a twelve-foot kite, was borne across a large brook and set down so frightened that he let the kite go.

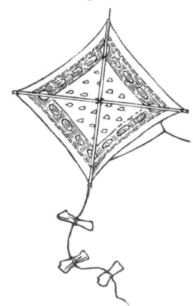

THE "BEN" FRANKLIN KITE.

In 1895 the western papers reported that a citizen of Winona, in exploiting a huge kite, was, by a gust of wind, jerked two hundred feet up in the air, then let down and ducked in the river.

But Ben Franklin did better than this; for once, while bathing, he caused his kite to draw him across the

5

river, thus saving himself the exertion of paddling and kicking.

BOYS' KITES.

The taste of the American boy does not usually run into such vagaries as the foregoing. He wants a kite that will operate in the same easy round, in its turn, with his base ball, his sled, his skates and his bow and arrow. There are several forms of these boys' kites which are easy to make and jolly to fly.

In making a kite there are three essentials,—strength, lightness and balance. The first two of these depend on the construction of the frame. Small tubes of thin steel, and also of aluminum, have been tried for this purpose, but have not given so good results as spruce wood. Next to this in strength, lightness and elasticity is whitewood, then straight-grained white pine. For small kites, strips of split bamboo will do very well; but they bend too easily if long. For bow kites or other curving forms, black ash or oak basket strips and split bamboo are good. Split rattan will not often prove satisfactory, because of its twist and its lack of uniform elasticity.

In selecting the material for a frame, care should be taken that the sticks are straight, with grain running in the direction of the length of the stick, and that the wood is thoroughly dry.

For a kite three feet long and two and a half feet wide, the *sticks* should be in the form of a slightly flattened square, not so thick as a common lead pencil,—that is, they should be *less* than half an inch wide and a quarter of an inch thick. The corners should not be rounded, but may be rubbed slightly to remove the sharpness.

The newspapers now made are not strong enough for kite coverings; thin, tough manila being the only cheap paper which is suitable. Bond paper, nainsook muslin and tracing cloth are also good; but the cheapest

6

of them is more than twice as costly as manila paper. Tissue paper makes a good covering for kites not over three feet in length,— if they can be kept away from all bushes and stubble, which would rend them into tatters in short order.

Very thin Chinese silk makes one of the best coverings for flying in brisk winds, which hold it in place; but in light winds (when the covering is properly loose) the fulness is given to sliding from one side to the other, thus destroying the balance of the kite.

To prepare a kite for flying in wet weather, cloth coverings should be varnished, and paper ones should be saturated with melted paraffine wax brushed on lightly and evenly. The paper in these should be folded from back to front,— the reverse of the folding of the margin for fair-weather flyers. Oiled silk is also good. These treatments, by closing the spaces between the threads, prevent the wind from passing through the covering, so that the lifting power of the kite is increased; but, because of the added weight, the kite will not ascend as readily in light winds. Only paper and the thinnest silk are light enough for small kites; but a four-foot kite would bear a nainsook muslin or a thin silesia in a fresh and steady wind.

The color of kite coverings is worth considering. Black is the color most easily distinguished at all heights. The changes of color in the sky are quite curious.

Dark blue, in a cloudy sky, appears black, but regains its color partially in sunshiny spaces.

Cherry red against a blue sky is usually surrounded by its complementary color in the form of fringes extending from its edges. The color darkens at great heights, but at a certain angle to the sun-rays it shows to the eye its real color.

Light green becomes invisible at a less height than pale blue.

A paper kite covering which had received one application of a buff stain — which proved insufficient to saturate the paper — showed a soiled green tint in the sunshine.

THE FRAME OF A KITE.

A kite whose width is less than three fourths of its length is rarely a good flyer. If a kite is to be furnished with a tail, the cross-stick may be placed as low as midway of the height, but the further the cross-stick is from the top (below a seventeenth of the length of the kite), the more wind resistance will it require in the tail. The two sticks should be bound together with one or two turns of small, hard twine in each of the four corners. No notches should be cut here, as these would weaken the sticks too much. When the covering is on the frame and the paste has become quite dry, the kite should be tested for balance. To obtain this it may be necessary to slip the cross-stick one way or the other through its binding. When a balance of the two sides of the kite is obtained (which can be done by suspending it from a cord rising from the backbone near the crossing) the binding of the two sticks should be tightened sufficiently to prevent any more slipping. The kite will fly better in strong winds if the cross-piece is bent like a bow, the convex side downward. The bow form may be retained in a straight-grained stick by a cord applied as a bow-string.

Bad behavior in the kite is quite sure to follow any twist in the sticks which renders the shape of the kite irregular; and in the Malay kite, whether of bow or keel cross-piece, any difference in the curves of the latter on the two sides will have the same result.

A coating of shellac varnish causes frames to retain their proper shape better when they are flown in a damp atmosphere. A coating of the varnish is also an advantage to any part of the kite where glue has been used, for a similar reason.

The cord which goes about the circumference of the kite should be as strong as the string by which the flyer holds the kite, and, if larger, might be a little softer without harm. This cord, passing from end to end of each stick, is fastened by a half knot in a notch at the end of each, the knot being on the front or downward side of the kite when flying, the same side which is to be covered. The notches should not be more than one fourth of an inch from the end of the stick, except at the lower end, where about one inch should be left to fasten the tail on.

When the frame is complete it is to be laid on the covering, which should be marked about one inch outside of the bounding cord. The frame should then be removed and the two sides of the paper below the cross-stick cut at the line marked. The frame is then placed on the paper again and the margins folded closely over the cord and made to adhere to the paper inside by a paste.

Home-made flour paste will serve, bookbinder's paste is better, stationers' mucilage is not so good as the last, but *good* liquid glue is best of all.

When it is found that the frame is properly set in the covering the two sides above the cross-piece are to be similarly marked and cut and pasted down on the side next the frame, also. The covering should be drawn straight on the length, but loose from side to side. It has been found that kites fly better with this slackness. It is easy to secure it uniformly over the kite by *crinkling* the covering thoroughly. This is usually done by crushing it into a ball with the hands, but without any rubbing. The paper that will not stand this treatment without perceptible weakening is not strong enough for kite covering.

The form of kite whose construction has just been described is known as the Common Diamond, or Cross Kite, which now only needs a bridle and a tail to render it ready for use. In this kite one end of the bridle (to which the kite string or holding cord is attached) is to be tied in a slight notch in the longer stick about half-

9

way between the cross-stick and the top, and the other end is attached similarly near to but not quite at the lower end. In some instances, however, owing to a peculiarity in the balance, it has been found better to fasten one

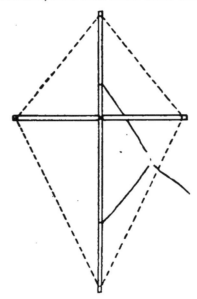

FRAME OF COMMON DIAMOND OR CROSS KITE.

end of the loop at the cross-stick and the other end near the lower point of the kite. This is the arrangement of the bridle in the Malay, Eddy and Keel Kites. The slack of the loop should be almost but not quite sufficient to reach either end of the cross-stick. The flying cord (that held by the person flying the kite) should be fastened to the loop, usually about one third its length from the upper fastening. This bridle necessarily passes through the covering of the kite at each fastening, and

10

it is best to paste a small disk of thin leather or tough paper about each hole to prevent cutting of the covering by the bridle cord.

THE KITE TAIL.

The tails used on kites vary from two to twenty times the length of the kite, according to the form and size of the latter, and to the size and nearness of the bobs. For a three-and-a-half-foot kite these should be made from stiff paper four or five inches long and almost as wide, tied at the middle in the kite cord, and about their length apart. At the end of the tail there should be a bob of double size in the form of a tassel.

Another form is the tail of cloth or paper cups or cones strung on a cord. This form is the invention of Mr. E. Douglass Archibald, an accomplished English meteorologist and aeronaut. These cones are placed on the tail with their larger ends towards the kite, the string being knotted about the small end to hold them in position; also, to two strings crossing the top, or large end. The top of the cup, if not of firm enough material to hold its circular form, may be stiffened by a hoop of thin basketing or of bookbinders' wire.

Five of these cups two inches in diameter are sufficient for a six or a seven foot kite. A single large cone at the end of several feet of cord has been found sufficient to steady an unruly six-foot Malay kite. The use of any kind of tail is in holding the kite steady. The proper proportions between the size and length of tail and kite is a matter of experiment in every case. In the scientific kite-flying the cup or cone has been found far the best. The weight of the tail and the pull of the wind on it take just that amount from the lifting power of the kite.

THE KITE STRING,

or operating cord, should be strong but small, the latter because of the very considerable pressure of the wind against it. This greatly increases the sag of the cord,

11

and its pull both on the kite and the holder of the
string.

The best cord for this purpose is of hard-twisted
flax, though in wet weather silk or linen fish-line is preferred by some for small kites. For those of less than

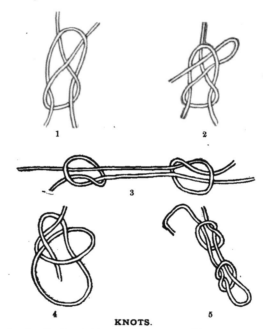

KNOTS.

1—Bowline Knot.   2—Bowline Knot arranged for easy untying.
3—Surgeon's Knot.   4—Bowstring Knot.
5—Running Knot with a check knot to hold.

five feet in length No. 9 hard-twisted flax will prove a
good article; for larger kites, up to nine feet, No. 18 is
suitable. The first is sold in balls containing about
two hundred yards, usually at the price of ten cents. A

ball of No. 9 weighs about five ounces for each 100 feet, and it will break at a pull of from 75 to 90 pounds.

All kite-flyers will need to learn to tie knots that will not slip. Some simple forms of knot, therefore, are shown by the diagram.

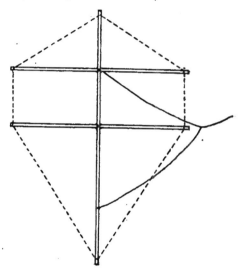

FRAME FOR A FORM OF HOUSE KITE.

Some persons in flying large kites insert a section of stronger cord next the kite, to guard against breakage in sudden gusts, while others prefer a piece of large elastic cord.

FLYING KITES.

Sometimes a kite will fly directly into the sky from the flyer's hand; but the conditions for this good behavior are a perfectly balanced kite and a steady breeze. The latter can only be found in an elevated, open situation ·

free from buildings, trees and other large, high masses. In ordinary conditions a supply of string must be laid out along the ground,—a length of fifty or a hundred feet being sometimes needed,—and the one holding the string must stand in such position that he can run against the wind for many yards; but a downhill course is generally unfavorable to the rise of the kite.

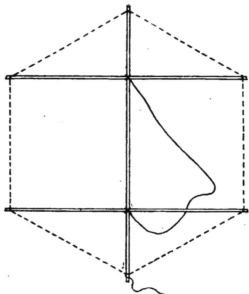

FRAME FOR ANOTHER FORM OF HOUSE KITE.
The dimensions of this design are one quarter wider than usual.

At a signal, the person carrying the kite, grasping it at the lower end, should give it a quick upward thrust against the wind, letting it go from his grasp on the instant. At the same time the one holding the string pulls it straight, and then — unless the kite is going upward steadily — retires against the wind, letting out more string as the kite climbs upward.

The kite should float at an angle of forty-five to fifty-five degrees; and it may be found necessary to knot the string to a different part of the bridle to obtain the

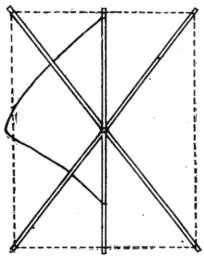

FORM OF RECTANGULAR KITE.

The middle stick may be omitted and the bridle attached to strings stretched, one above, the other below the crossing, or to one of the sticks.

best angle for the wind. Only practice will teach this. Attaching a bridle to the cross-piece — fastening the flying cord to both as they cross — has sometimes been found an advantage with large kites in gusty winds.

Often before reaching a stratum of steady wind, even a very good kite will sometimes take a sudden dodge, and may even descend to earth, if not checked, which can generally be done by letting out string. When the kite has again taken a proper position it can be sent upward by a judicious pulling in of the string. As soon as the kite is under good headway again it should be given more string, but not so fast as to allow it to slacken its pull. When this occurs the string should be quickly drawn taut.

When the kite has gone up as high as the weight of the string will let it, another kite may be sent up with fifty or more feet of line of its own (according to size) attached to the main line to help lift it, when both kites

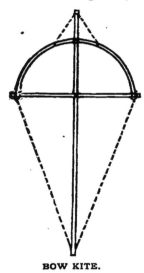

BOW KITE.

will go higher than one alone. This action may be repeated to the extent of several kites, if the main line be strong enough to hold. The spaces on the latter between the kite connections should be from sixty to a hundred feet,— the larger the lower kite the greater should be the distance. The more kites there are on a line the steadier is its pull.

16

It is found that large kites can be more safely relied upon to fly than small ones, probably on the same principle that a small boat tosses wildly on waves where a ship would ride steadily.

KITE DECORATIONS.

Practice in kite-flying will soon lead to devices for increasing its interest. One of the easiest is the messenger. This is a stiff piece of paper from three to six inches in diameter, of various forms, and having in the

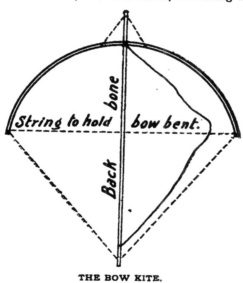

THE BOW KITE.

centre a hole much larger than the string, upon which it is slipped by a slit. It should not be put on the string until the kite is well poised in the sky, when the wind will whirl the messenger along the cord up to the kite. Another would be some kind of æolian attachment, or a

17

tiny bell suspended at the bottom of the kite, also at the ends of the frame if the kite will sustain the weight. Thus the kite-flyer can ring his chimes in the sky many times higher than the steeples.

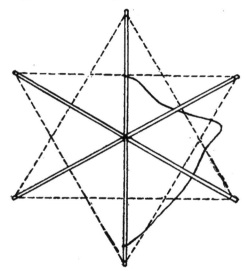

FRAME OF STAR KITE.

The three heavy lines are the sticks; the broken lines represent the string which forms the outline of the kite.

Streamers of colored paper attached to the angles have a pleasing effect, and paper figures suspended from the kite and from the messenger are very amusing in their antics.

KITES OF MANY SHAPES.

The Common Diamond, or Cross Kite, was described in the instructions for making frames and covering them.

18

To make a Regular Diamond Kite the two sticks should be crossed at the middle; but the form does not possess good flying qualities.

The House Kite is made by putting a second cross-piece of the same length at the same distance from the lower end of the kite as the upper one is from the top.

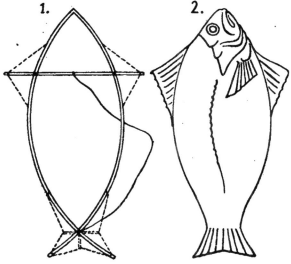

FISH KITE.

If these cross-pieces be carried quite to the end of the sticks we have a Long Rectangular Kite. The same form may be obtained with less weight by crossing two sticks of the same length at the middle and connecting the ends by a cord.

If these two sticks be of equal length and crossed at right angles we have a Square Kite.

In the Round Kite a light hoop constitutes the frame, which should be braced in one direction by a slender stick, at the ends of which the bridle is to be fastened.

The Elliptical Kite differs only in construction from the last in having for a brace a stick longer than the diameter of the hoop.

One form of the Bow-top Kite has a stiff strip of basketing instead of a cord extending from end to end

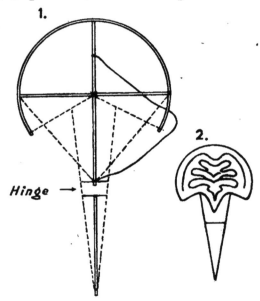

KING (OR HORSESHOE) CRAB KITE.

of the cross-piece, over the top, where it is pegged, or, being slit, is pressed down to a shoulder cut in the top of the backbone.

If the end of the latter extends two or three inches above the bow, and a cord is run from the top of it to the

MAN-FORM KITE.

bow obliquely on each side, a Peaked Kite is formed. A lighter form of the Bow Kite has no cross-piece, the bounding cords extending from the ends of the bow to the lower end of the backbone. In this form the bow must have a degree of stiffness that could only be found in a piece of wood three or four times the thickness of that needed with the cross-stick.

BALLOON KITES.

Any kite here mentioned, except those of the Hargrave type, may be turned into a wind balloon by being furnished with a covering on the back or upward side. The rotundity will, of course, depend on the degree of slackness of the back covering. This should be very light and pliable. Tissue paper would serve excellently were it strong enough, but it is apt to burst from the

21

BOY KITE.

The heavy line represents the sticks, the broken lines the bounding and bracing cords.

Loops of basket strips at the end of the arms may be formed to receive gloves, or hands cut from paper board may be substituted. The feet also should be of paper board, and, if attached loosely, will have lively action in the air.

pressure of the wind. Japanese paper (not often met with except in the form of handkerchiefs or napkins) would be much better. The wind is admitted through one or more holes in the front covering near the centre of the kite. The diameter of these apertures should not be more than an inch to a foot of the kite's width. It is necessary to have a vent for the wind in the balloon covering to avoid its bursting in gusts. This should be at the bottom of the kite and of equal capacity with the wind inlets. This form, properly made, is a better flyer than the common kite.

22

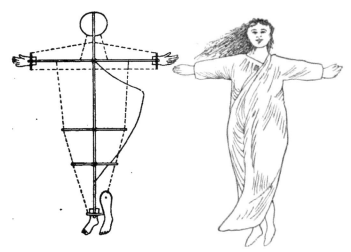

A GOOD FLYER.

For Kite Nymph,—hair, strips of tissue paper; hands and feet, paper or leather board. The paper used on covering should be crinkled and very loose, with free ends at the bottom. With the proper form of covering this frame will serve equally well for a male figure. Heavy lines, sticks; dotted lines, string.

CHINESE KITES.

The Dragon Kite of the Chinese usually consists of a large roundish disk, followed by smaller disks, in two lines, connected by cords to the head and by other cords to each other. A transverse bamboo twig, or a rod with sprigs of plumy grass at the ends, is affixed to each side of the small disks. The surface of the large foremost disk is decorated with a face, in bright colors, and often of most hideous appearance. The disks gradually decrease in size from head to tail, ending in a pair of streamers. The line assumes an undulatory movement, presenting much of the appearance of a crawling ser-

23

pent. Great skill is required to launch these kites in the air. It is said that they are regarded by the China-men as defenders; their great ugliness of appearance being supposed to frighten away invisible enemies.

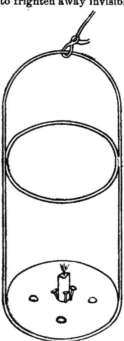

FRAME OF LANTERN TO BE SUSPENDED FROM KITE.
Openings should be left at top and bottom for draught.

Chinese kites, especially those in bird forms, are often furnished with a resonator, formed of a section of bamboo, of which a hollow constitutes about one half or more the diameter for the whole length. It has three apertures,—one at each end and one at the middle.

24

The tones are strong and plaintive, and may be heard a long distance.

Various tones may be obtained by varying the form of the resonator as to the size of the cavity and of the holes entering it, their number and proportion. The

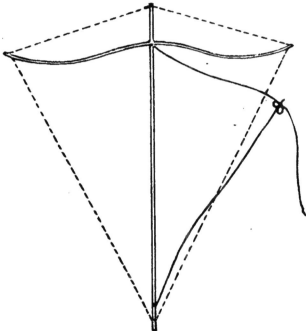

FRAME FOR MALAY KITE.

resonator may be of any material, and be applied to any form of kite which is sufficiently large and light to sustain its weight. Tongues of metal or of bamboo are also often attached to kites in such a way as to receive the wind and afford a variety of pleasing tones.

There is an idea prevalent among Chinamen that these musical kites also keep evil spirits away. Sometimes their strings are fastened on the roofs, and the kites kept in the air for many days and nights in succession; the family feeling entirely secure as long as the music can be heard aloft.

JAPANESE KITES.

The people of Japan are also greatly addicted to kite-flying, but with them it is more of a social festivity for friends and neighbors. Variety of form is a

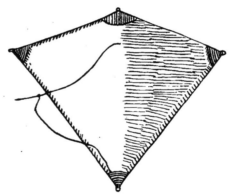

THE EDDY KITE.
Front view, showing the covering.

characteristic of Japanese kites, which rudely imitate familiar animals, birds and fishes. Often these different forms, like the totems of American Indian tribes, are the recognized token of some individual or family; so that a person to whom the appearance of the kites of a village is familiar can recognize them at a distance, and learn whether certain acquaintances are at the other end of the line enjoying a holiday.

TAILLESS KITES.

Of the old Oriental forms of the kite the only one which has gained the approval of scientific men is that flown on the Malay Peninsula. Though without a tail, it has a beautiful appearance in the air. Its breadth is above three fourths of its length, and is greatest quite near the top, like the so-called Eddy bird-form kite. Its other notable feature is the cross-piece, which has the shape of a Cupid's bow, the convex middle portion being downward, in the same direction with the curving tips.

There is a common idea of the inexperienced that a kite flown with the frame side down will fly better, because the balloon-like expansion of the covering which

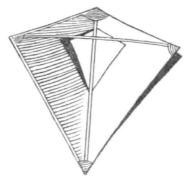

THE EDDY KITE.

A storm-flyer. The diamond-shaped figure in the centre is an opening made to lessen the wind pressure.

would occur in this position, it is reasoned, would hold the wind, and that the kite would thus be better supported than in the reverse position. In practice this has always been found fallacious. A kite thus mounted is given to cavorting around in a circle with the lower end

27

of the string as an axis, rarely ascending high enough to clear the ground when it dives, and inevitably dropping to earth at a lull in the wind. With the convex side downward, on the contrary, when the wind (as it usually does every other instant) pushes on one side of the kite a little harder than on the other, the convexity allows it to slide off, the kite tipping barely enough to be observed. This action on one side is instantly repeated on the other; so that almost always convex kites have a wavy motion, which is so nearly simultaneous on both sides as to give transient beholders the impression of a floating gull or albatross that slightly waves its wings in happy triumph over the unstable element of air.

THE EDDY KITE.

This is a modification of the Malay kite, more for use than for beauty; yet it has an attractive appearance in the air, and the action of a flight of them is almost as pleasing as that of its Oriental prototype. The height and breadth of this kite are equal, the cross-piece being

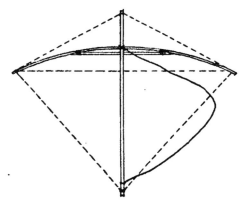

FRAME AND STRINGING OF TAILLESS KITE.
Showing strengthening cross-piece.

28

PHOTOGRAPHING FROM A KITE LINE.

29

only about one eighteenth of the kite's length from the top. It is very simple in its construction, the two sticks being tied across each other, the ends of the cross-stick bent upward, bow-like, by means of a string. A stick of nearly equal size, but only one fourth to one third as long, is placed on the opposite side of the kite's spine, and the ends bound to the cross-piece. This serves both to strengthen the latter and to improve the balance of the kite by an adjustment indicated by tentative flights. The average weight of a six-foot kite is one pound, and for light winds it should be less.

This kite was the invention or production of Mr. William A. Eddy of Bayonne, N. J.; who has sent his kites up not only from the vicinity of his home, but in New York, Boston and other cities, mainly for the purpose of making bird's-eye views with the camera.

Until recently the statement that photography might be done in the air by the instrument sustained by kites would have subjected the proposer to ridicule as a flighty enthusiast or to a suspicion of incipient insanity. The feat of producing a good picture by such means appears to have been first performed by Messrs. G. T. Woglom and George E. Henshaw of New York City, on the afternoon of Sept. 21, 1895. Such pictures are now frequently made by several different amateur and professional aeronauts.

Doubtless there are persons of wandering habit who would feel less safe were they aware that the gaze of this "eye in the sky" might at any time be directed on them; but there are also many others who would really be safer were it known that the kite-camera was abroad in the land.

The flat kites used for photographing purposes are generally of the dimensions of five and seven feet respectively. From three to seven of these, according to the strength and steadiness of the wind, are necessary to carry the camera to a proper height and sustain it with the least degree of motion. The instrument is

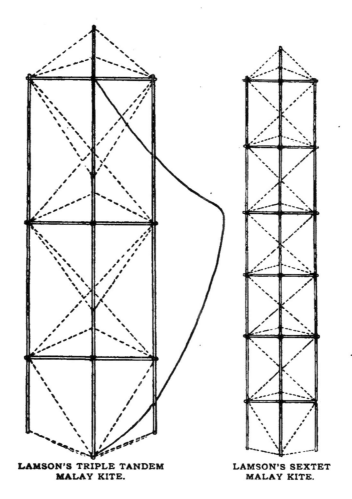

**LAMSON'S TRIPLE TANDEM
MALAY KITE.**

**LAMSON'S SEXTET
MALAY KITE.**

31

mounted at the angle of two slender poles, the end of one of which is attached to the middle of the other. Cords from one or more trunk lines fasten to the three outward ends of the poles, and the direction of the instrument is by this means controlled. The camera is operated by a special string.

In Mr. Eddy's practice, the main line, to which the branch strings are knotted, is carried on a large reel running in a box that is securely fastened down. This cord is of about the diameter of a common lead pencil.

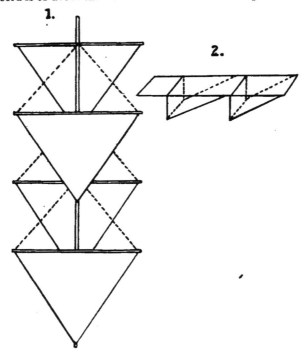

1.

2.

LAMSON'S MULTIPLE FOLDING KITES.

A hundred feet of such cord weighs about a pound, more of a load than a small kite could carry-up. The wind, of course, causes a very large additional sag in a string offering so much surface, greatly increasing the pull both on the kites and the ground connection.

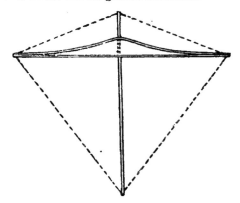

FRAME OF KEEL KITE (BLUE HILL OBSERVATORY).

THE BLUE HILL KITES.

Sometimes Mr. Eddy sends up a thermometer, but this kind of work is less in his line than in that of the scientific corps at the Blue Hill Observatory, who take kite observations of the atmosphere almost every day at certain seasons.*

At first the meteorological instruments were sent up in a basket; but now they have a curious aluminum box one foot high, the same on one side, and six inches in the other dimension. Its weight, including the instru-

---

*The Blue Hill Observatory is situated on Blue Hill, an elevation of 635 feet, in a southern suburb of Boston. Its purpose is chiefly the observation of the weather and the investigation of the atmosphere. It is owned and sustained by Mr. A. Lawrence Rotch, of Boston, from philanthropic motives.

ments, is about three pounds. In it, and part of it, is a cylinder revolving by clock-work which takes the varying record of each instrument,— a thermal indicator, barometer, a hygrometer and an anemometer; so that when this "meteorograph" is drawn down there are found, in ink lines, the progressive record of the temperature, the weight and the moisture of the atmosphere, the velocity of the wind, and the altitude of the ascent.

Plainly made Malay kites are much used at Blue Hill. A form of keel kite invented by Mr. Clayton of the Observatory, now in use at Blue Hill, has a frame of

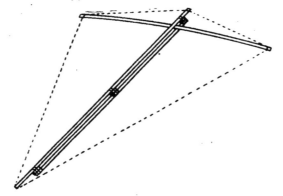

FRAME OF THE CLAYTON KEEL KITE.

straight sticks, with an extra stick trussed on the backbone, between that and the covering, by which the latter is raised along the middle into a considerable ridge for nearly the whole length of the kite. This is regarded as a superior kite. A cell kite constructed on the cell and parallel plane system is also much used at Blue Hill, being a modification of the Hargrave kite.

Two of the Hargrave kites, on Nov. 12, 1894, in Australia, lifted the inventor, Mr. Hargrave, sixteen feet

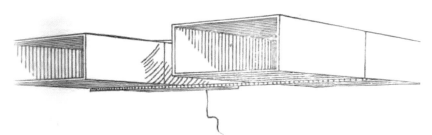

THE HARGRAVE BOX KITE (Later Form).

from the ground; and in 1895 he was lifted forty feet by the same means.

This form, to the uninitiated, does not suggest a kite at all. It consists of a light wooden frame several feet in length, having a width of nearly one third its length, and a depth of about half the width. All except the ends is covered with thin cloth of close texture. It is usually flown in pairs, the two kites being connected by

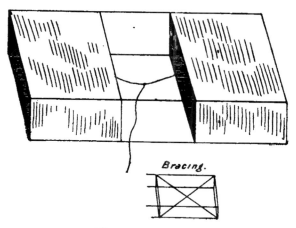

Bracing.

THE CLAYTON KITE.

35

a light wooden bar fastened across the middle of each below, and another bar above. The two kites are placed about the depth of one apart. The string is usually attached midway of the bars.

The box kite, invented by Mr. H. H. Clayton of the Blue Hill Observatory, differs from the foregoing chiefly in having nearly one third of the box, at the middle, without covering, so that in this section the four corner bars of the frame are visible and the space open to the wind. This kite goes up readily, at a short, quick lift on the cord, followed by a steady pull. It ascends to high altitudes, floats steadily, and is a good lifter. This kind is usually preferred for observations with the instruments in violent weather. Mr. Clayton has a large kite

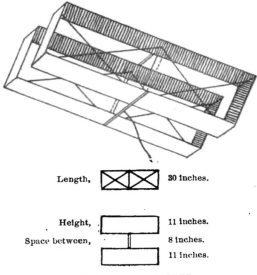

Length, 30 inches.

Height, 11 inches.
Space between, 8 inches.
11 inches.

EARLY HARGRAVE KITE.

This sometimes assumes an angle of 55 degrees.

of this pattern which he thinks would, in a good wind, take up a man of average size.

The lifting of Mr. Hargrave is not a solitary example of this feat in scientific exploiting. Subsequently Capt. H. Baden-Powell, of the Scotch Grays, in England, was lifted one hundred feet from the ground by kites. He was provided with a parachute for safety in case the kites broke.

On Jan. 21, 1897, in the vicinity of New York Bay, Lieut. Hugh D. Wise, of the Ninth Infantry, U. S. A., was lifted in a boatswain's swing suspended from four kites in double tandem, to a height of forty-two feet. The dimensions of these kites are not readily accessible; but from their total weight — which we have — of sixty-five pounds, they must have been very large, even for the Hargrave pattern.

Frequent use is made at Blue Hill of the cup or cone tail for steadying the Malay kites, especially in variable winds or when the parts of the kite are poorly balanced. Two cones six inches in greatest diameter worked well on a six-foot kite; and one eight inches in diameter, at the end of fifteen feet of string, also did well.

The flat kites used at Blue Hill vary in size from four to nine feet. Both paper and cloth are used for coverings. The largest size furnishes about sixty-five feet of wind-surface. As many as a dozen kites, including those of nine, seven and four feet, have been flown at once from the same main line. The lift on the cord in a brisk breeze is not to be despised; it has sometimes been as much as three strong men could control, and was found to be very exhausting labor.

In the summer of 1896 the string of vegetable fibre for a trunk or main line was discarded and the smallest size of piano string adopted instead. It is of No. 14 steel wire, and two and one eighth miles of it weigh but twelve pounds. This is lighter than the bulky flaxen cord, and offers much less resistance to the wind, so that two kites with this string will ascend and bear the instru-

37

ments to as great a height as three times as many with the clumsy cord of vegetable fibre.

Under the strain on the cord more than one reel of solid oak has been crushed, and with increased skill in flying so that a larger number of kites were sent to loftier altitudes, stronger and stronger reeling apparatus had to be provided. Through the year 1896 the string was wound in or run out from a huge spool mounted on

GETTING OBSERVATIONS FROM KITES AT BLUE HILL OBSERVATORY. REEL AND AZIMUTH.

a strong, weighted frame, with a crank at each end for turning it; and, with this, two hours of hard work were ordinarily required to pull down even half a dozen of the kites. The string runs out and in under a grooved wheel in front of the spool. Connected with this wheel is a dial, by which the length of wire run out is accurately recorded and may be known at any moment. The whole apparatus is mounted on a heavy hand truck.

Even this has proved too laborious, and it became apparent that a less rigid delivering apparatus was a necessity for attaining the altitudes the Observatory people desired to reach with their instruments. Accordingly there was installed in the spring of 1897 a reel of ample size and strength, operated by a two-horse-power engine, this being supplied with steam from a boiler heated by burning kerosene spray. The entire apparatus is very compact. By the use of an endless screw a back-and-forth movement of the spool is obtained, by which the wire is drawn off or wound on directly in front of the adjusting guide, the grooved wheel being pivoted to turn any way to keep the direction of the kites. To prevent this steel wire from rusting, oil is dripped continually in the groove of the wheel as the string is wound in.

HEIGHT OF ASCENTS.

The highest ascent of a kite previous to the spring of 1897 was made on Oct. 8, 1896. Nine kites strung along the line lifted the wire. The top kite was a six-footer of the Malay (or Eddy) type. This rose 9,400 feet above the sea level, 9,300 feet above the surrounding country, or 8,770 feet above the top of Blue Hill. The flight of the first kite was therefore more than three thousand feet higher than the top of Mount Washington.

The instrument recording automatically temperature, humidity and air pressure was lifted 9,375 feet above sea level.

With the new reeling apparatus it is hoped that the meteorograph will be sent to a height of two miles, — which will require about four miles of wire.

SCIENTIFIC AND ECONOMICAL USES OF KITE-FLYING.

If one questions, What is the real value of all this practice with kites? the Observatory corps would doubtless reply: We are living in an atmosphere of which

39

we practically know very little. Our position is like that of crabs at the bottom of the sea. It is expected that such knowledge will be gained in these aerial explorations as will enable the meteorologist to predict hot and cold waves and the various kinds of storms more accurately and much earlier than has been done heretofore. The knowledge already obtained has modified opinions which have been expressed in text-books.

CURIOUS OBSERVATIONS.

The use of wire for a kite-string has also its drawbacks, one of which is the electricity, a phenomenon that rarely gave annoyance with the cord of vegetable fibre. The conduction of the wire between high strata of air and the earth rendered the work of those who manipulated the string quite torturing, until the device of a grounded section of stiff wire running on the string above the contact of the hands was introduced. Even now in handling the wire the men sometimes give a sudden start with a sharp exclamation when a mischievous boy kicks over the stone holding the ground wire down.

When three thousand or more feet of wire have been let out, a chain of short but frequent sparks issues from it almost constantly, and this as well in clear as in cloudy weather, the discharge being especially strong during snowstorms.

"The atmosphere," says Mr. Clayton, the chief of the corps, "appears to be an inexhaustible reservoir of electricity, and it is only necessary to tap it with a long enough line in any kind of weather, and a supply of electricity is at hand."

In the tests at Blue Hill the temperature almost always lowers as the altitudes increase, rising only in rare conditions. Observations by Mr. Eddy and by Chief Moore, of the United States Weather Bureau at Washington, also show that warm and cold waves are felt in the upper atmosphere from six to twelve hours earlier than they are felt in full strength at the solid surface of the earth. Apparently the reason is that air moves along much more rapidly above than at the earth's surface, where it is retarded by friction. In advance of and during cold waves from the west the temperature falls uniformly but very rapidly as the kites ascend, while in advance of warm waves the temperature as the kites rise first decreases, but increases suddenly when the tide of heated air is reached. In some cases the rise is as much as fifteen to seventeen degrees. It has been noted at Blue Hill that along this coast a cool flow of air from the east, on the contrary, begins at the surface of the earth, the tide gradually becoming deeper by increase in height.

Early one August afternoon, while a five-foot kite was aloft in a breeze so light as barely to keep it from falling, a large cumulus cloud approached the zenith. When directly above the kite the latter began to ascend rapidly and almost vertically, only ceasing when its string was all out and drawn taut. The kite followed the course of the cloud across the sky as far as the string would permit, and when it had fully passed, rapidly fell to its former position.

At another time (July, 1896) the kites passed through a wide cloud, coming out in a clear sky above. In the midst of the cloud the humidity, as shown by the hygrometer, was one hundred per cent (full saturation,—as much as possible without precipitation), but above the cloud the air was found to be quite dry. A tolerably accurate measurement showed the cloud to be about five hundred feet in depth.

In spring and autumn, in such conditions, the kites and such portions of the strings as pass above the cloud, when drawn down, are often found to have a beautiful coating of minute water crystals.

In the ascent of Oct. 8, 1896, the instruments, at the elevation of three fourths of a mile, entered a cloud, emerging from it at the altitude of about one mile. Just beneath the cloud the temperature was below freezing, above it the air was very dry. At about 4.30 P. M., when the instruments were at the highest point reached (9,375 feet above sea level), a temperature of 20° below the freezing point was recorded.

Once an entire string of kites broke away and went off with the wind, carrying the instruments with them. They dropped from a height of 4,300 feet at the rate of 1,100 feet a minute, moving diagonally down. They landed in the Quincy woods, about three miles from the Observatory. The meteorograph was found to be uninjured, and the instruments were but slightly deranged by the escapade.

OTHER KITE FLYERS

in New York, Washington, Indianapolis and in England have been for several years pursuing in diverse ways and for dissimilar purposes these kite experiments. In England the motives of the different devotees of this branch of the science of aeronautics have been meteorological only, until recently; but for a couple of years some have pursued their experiments for military uses. Those at Blue Hill and those of the United States Weather Bureau officials at Washington and some other points have been for the purposes of science and peaceful economics. In the vicinity of New York the chief purposes of effort have been military, and economy of life and labor; the latter embracing flying kites with lines to wrecked vessels, sending lines to otherwise inaccessible points, as lofty crags, temporarily isolated bridge piers, and towers and steeples.

The military uses for which the development of kite-flying has been sought are bird's-eye photography; the raising of an observer high in air; the suspension of several miles of telegraph wire to pass a territory held by a hostile army; the flashing of sun-gleams, as signals from mirrors carried up by kites, to be read by observers at a post perhaps a hundred miles distant; and the raising of apparatus to give electric flashes for the same purpose in the dark hours.

Mr. S. A. Potter, of Washington, now sends his cellular kite to a height of a thousand feet in five minutes. He has recently made use of a new device in a supplementary cord, by which a kite can be controlled to a surprising extent. His kite is readily directed to and held at an angle of 60° with the wind on either side. Mr. Potter's experiments have taken a suggestive relation to aerial transportation — particularly the proposed system of floating cars held down and directed by a trolley line beneath them — which is under serious consideration in certain quarters. These experiments also have instruction for Professor Langley, of the Smithsonian Institute, and Mr. Hiram Maxim, of England, in their experiments with their planotype flying machines.

Mr. Potter's kite is a box-form, of regular diamond shape; the long axis being horizontal, the short axis vertical. Another experimenter, also of Washington, has recently improved on the Potter kite, by adding a wing on each side.

The approach of flying machines designed for the transportation of human freight through the invisible spaces of the sky warns us of the limits of this monograph; for its readers are supposed to prefer the flying of the giddy kite rather than personal exploration of the viewless heights in the chill and airless tracts up toward the empyrean.

CPSIA information can be obtained
at www.ICGtesting.com
Printed in the USA
422024LV00017B/123